Threatened Cultures

RAIN FOREST AMERINDIANS

Anna Lewington

RSVP

**RAINTREE
STECK-VAUGHN**
P U B L I S H E R S
The Steck-Vaughn Company

Austin, Texas

Titles in the Series

Australian Aborigines
Bedouin
Inuit
Rain Forest Amerindians

The author gratefully acknowledges the help of Survival International in the writing of this book.

Series editors: Paul Mason and Pam Wells
Designer: Kudos Editorial and Design Services

Picture acknowledgments
The artwork on page 5 was supplied by Peter Bull.
The publishers gratefully acknowledge the permission of the following to use their pictures: Sue Cunningham 7, 8, 9, 11, 15, 17, 18, 20, 21, 23, 24, 25, 30, 31, 32, 34, 35, 37, 38, 39, 42; The Gaia Foundation 43; Edward Parker 4, 10, 12, 13, 14, 16, 19, 25, 27, 28, 29, 33, 36, 40, 41(both), 45; Darrell Posey 22; Survival International 6, 44.

Library of Congress Cataloging-in-Publication Data
Lewington, Anna.
  Rain forest Amerindians / Anna Lewington.
    p. cm. — (Threatened cultures)
  Includes bibliographical references and index.
  Summary: Discusses the Amerindians and their continuing struggle to preserve their way of life and maintain their cultural identity in the modern world.
  ISBN 0-8114-2302-6
  1. Indians of South America—Amazon River Valley—Juvenile literature.
2. Human ecology—Amazon River Valley—Juvenile literature. 3. Indians of South America—Brazil—Government relations—Juvenile literature. [1. Indians of South America—Amazon River Valley. 2. Human ecology—Amazon River Valley. 3. Amazon River Valley. 4. Rain forests.] I. Title. II. Title: Rain forest Amerindians. III. Series.
F2519.1.A6L49 1993
981'.1—dc20
                                                                    92-10560
                                                                    CIP AC

Printed by Lego, Italy
Bound in the United States by Lake Book, Melrose Park, IL

1 2 3 4 5 6 7 8 9 0 LB 98 97 96 95 94 93

Contents

1 Introduction

The Amazon rain forest is the home of many different peoples. The Amerindians have lived there the longest. Their ancestors settled in the forest thousands of years ago. Today, about one million Amerindians live there, in territory that is divided between Brazil, Peru, Ecuador, Colombia, Bolivia, Venezuela, French Guiana, Guyana, and Suriname.

When Europeans arrived in South America 500 years ago, it is believed that twelve to fifteen million Amerindians were living in the Amazon basin. This vast region, shaped by the mighty Amazon River and its tributaries, covers an area of about 2,300,000 square miles. It is made up of immense areas of tropical forest, in addition to open grasslands.

▲   The Amazon rain forest is the home of over 500 different peoples.

AMERINDIAN LANDS

This map shows the location of the Amerindian lands mentioned in this book.

CENTRAL AMERICA

PANAMA

TRINIDAD AND TOBAGO

VENEZUELA

GUYANA

FRENCH GUIANA

SURINAME

COLOMBIA

Equator

Manaus

Amazon

ECUADOR

PERU

B R A Z I L

Brasília

BOLIVIA

PACIFIC OCEAN

São Paulo

Rio de Janeiro

PARAGUAY

URUGUAY

ARGENTINA

CHILE

ATLANTIC OCEAN

1.	Aguaruna	26.	Pankaruru
2.	Amuesha	27.	Piaroa
3.	Arara	28.	Quichua
4.	Arawete	29.	Secoya
5.	Ashaninka	30.	Shipibo
6.	Asurini	31.	Shuar
7.	Chimane	32.	Siona
8.	Cinta Larga	33.	Surui
9.	Cofan	34.	Ticuna
10.	Cuiva	35.	Tukano
11.	Gavioes	36.	Uru Eu Wau Wau
12.	Guaja	37.	Waimiri-Atroari
13.	Huambisa	38.	Waorani
14.	Juruna	39.	Witoto
15.	Kaingang	40.	Xavante
16.	Kararao-Kayapo	41.	Xicrin-Kayapo
17.	Kayapo	42.	Yagua
18.	Krenak	43.	Yanomami
19.	Macuxi	44.	Yuki
20.	Matsigenka		
21.	Mehinaku		
22.	Nahua		
23.	Nambiquara		
24.	Panare		
25.	Parakana		

◀ The red color on this Kayapo man's face comes from *annatto* seeds.

As more Europeans came to the Amazon, most of them wanted to conquer, use, or change the forest and its indigenous people, the Amerindians, in some way. They brought diseases like malaria, chicken pox, and measles, in addition to the common cold, to which the Amerindians had no resistance. These diseases killed thousands of Amerindians, but many others were simply murdered. It is for these reasons that so few Amerindians are left today.

In the last twenty years the governments of most Amazonian countries have encouraged great numbers of people to move into the forest. They have destroyed large areas of trees and have often clashed with the Amerindian groups to whom the land belongs.

Other settlers, like the *caboclos* whose families married Amerindians long ago, and the rubber tappers, who have lived in the forest for several generations, have not destroyed the trees. They have learned from the Amerindians how to use the forest without harming it.

To the Amerindians the rain forest is much more than the rivers, trees, and animals that make it up. For thousands of years it has given them everything they need, and they think of the forest as a parent or grandparent, nourishing and teaching them, and forming the way they think about the world. Amerindians feel that they belong to the forest, since they have looked after it and helped to shape it. Without the forest, life has little meaning for them.

Today Amerindians are trying to stop others from destroying the Amazon rain forest, not just for their children and grandchildren, but for all of us, wherever we may live.

2

Rain Forest People

There are at least 500 different Amerindian peoples – or nations, as they prefer to be called – living in the Amazon rain forest today. Their societies all vary, and they live in groups of many kinds. In some, just a few families live together or near each other. In others, many families live in large communities of several thousand individuals, spread out across large areas of forest or grassland.

Usually, the names that different peoples use for themselves, like Waorani or Matsigenka, simply mean "us" or "people who live in a certain place." The names they give their traditional territories often mean "our land."

◀ This Mehinaku man is a member of one of the sixteen different peoples who live in the Xingu National Park. Behind him you can see the large communal house he shares.

▲ A traditional Kayapo village surrounded by forest and gardens.

Different languages, beliefs, and traditions distinguish the peoples of the rain forest. The Kayapo are just one of these.

THE KAYAPO

The Kayapo people live in eastern Brazil in the region of the Xingu River. They number about 3,500 individuals in all, divided into different subgroups. There are fourteen main communities or villages, some located towards the north and some to the south of the Xingu River. The largest village, Gorotire, has over 720 people.

Traditional Kayapo villages are built in the form of a circle of wooden houses with palm-leaf thatched roofs, with one or more larger houses in the center. While men, women, and children live in the circle of family houses, only the men use the central house. It is a special place for them to meet together socially, to plan for the future, and make political decisions that will affect the whole village.

Instead of having separate gardens or backyards (as most Westerners do), all the families in the villages share the forest and savanna land that is traditionally theirs. The Kayapo hunt wild animals and many kinds of birds. Families also keep many different animals as pets. People catch fish and crustaceans in the rivers and streams. But they are always careful not to catch too many birds or fish or other animals. They know that if they do there will be fewer to feed their children in the future.

LIVING WITH PLANTS AND ANIMALS

Like other Amerindian peoples, the Kayapo have a detailed understanding of every part of their environment. The Kayapo's forest and savanna land contain countless different plants. Just a small patch of forest, two and one-half acres in size, might contain around 100 different species of tree. But the forest did not become as diverse as this all on its own. Amerindians have helped to make the forest as complex and varied as it is. Over the thousands of years they have been living there they have been selecting and planting useful trees and shrubs. So the whole of their forest is like a huge wild garden.

The Kayapo have at least one use for 90 percent of the plants which grow around their villages. These include plants for food, medicines, building materials, and for dress and decoration.

THE RAIN FOREST GARDEN

As well as gathering and collecting many of the things they need, Kayapo families plant fruit trees and vegetable crops along the forest trails they use. They make gardens in forest clearings every year. Some groups also make "islands" of useful forest trees and plants in the savanna land, so that they will have extra supplies of food and medicines and somewhere to rest when they are out on a journey.

Like most other Amerindians, they grow a large number of crops, including many varieties of manioc, maize, sweet potatoes, pineapples, peppers, beans and yams. Though the soils are often very poor, Kayapo women especially are expert forest managers. They cultivate gardens in different forest and savanna zones in a very careful and organized way, improving the soil at the same time. They understand exactly what will make each plant grow well and make special fertilizers out of plant leaves, ashes, and termites' nests. Mixtures of plants are grown in groupings

Color from the Rain Forest

The Kayapo, in common with most other Amerindian peoples, use face and body paint to indicate important things about themselves. The designs and color combinations that are used may reflect the sex and status of a person (whether a small child, an experienced hunter or a widowed woman) and are especially worn for rituals and ceremonies.

Different peoples have developed particular designs which distinguish them, but most incorporate the colors red and black. Both of these are made from plants. The juice pressed from the green fruits of the stately *genipapo* tree (*Genipa americana*) makes a deep blue-black color. The orange-red is usually made from the waxy outer coating of seeds from the *annatto* tree (*Bixa orellana*).

they call "friends who grow together" because the Kayapo know that many will do better like this. Some plants protect others, for example, not just by sheltering them from the fierce tropical sun and torrential rain, but preventing attack from insects or smothering by weeds.

Certain kinds of banana trees are often planted around Kayapo crops. The wasps that make their nests among the banana leaves attack the ants that try to eat the crops. The Kayapo also select plants with important qualities, like good flavor and resistance to disease. Each family, from generation to generation, is responsible for cultivating and improving a useful plant.

After three to four years forest gardens are left to grow wild, but the Kayapo still come back to harvest fruit from mature trees and collect medicinal plants. Like other traditional Amerindians, they have an excellent diet. Around the year they can choose from about 250 types of fruit, as well as hundreds of different vegetables, nuts, and leaves. They are especially fond of honey and have domesticated nine species of stingless bees. Medicines are made from many of the 650 medicinal plants they are familiar with.

THE SHARING SOCIETY

Sharing and exchange are basic to Amerindians. They believe that they must cooperate with each

▲ Amerindians have helped to make the forest as varied as it is by planting many different kinds of trees.

▲ Although Kayapo villages have chiefs, these men guide others by discussion rather than telling them what to do. Here, Chief Raoni discusses a point with other elders.

other and with all the plants and creatures in the forest. Respect for living things is fundamental to their way of life and is marked by special ceremonies and festivals.

Although each village has at least one chief, these men guide others by discussion and persuasion. When people marry, they choose someone from a different kin group or village, and this unites not just the couple but the groups as well. Parties are held and trade goods exchanged between these groups. In this way important alliances are made.

PROTECTING THE LAND

When problems arise, alliances are very important, enabling people to come together to find solutions as a team. The Kayapo's biggest problem is protecting their land. Settlers from other parts of Brazil have entered their territory illegally and destroyed large areas of trees. Ranchers and farmers would like to take over the Kayapo grasslands, which would destroy many of the plants and animals the Kayapo need. Hydroelectric projects on the Xingu River have threatened to flood Kayapo forest land.

The Kayapo chief Paulinho Paiakan has said :

"We are fighting to defend the forest. It is because the forest is what makes us, and what makes our hearts go."

Amerindian Lands

3

Amerindian lands are spread throughout the Amazon region. This huge area, which extends into nine countries, is nearly as big as the U.S. and twenty-eight times the size of Britain. From the air, the Amazon rain forest looks very flat — an endless carpet of treetops in different shades of green. Over 1,000 tributaries of the Amazon River thread their way through this great expanse of vegetation.

Most of the land is less than 1000 feet above sea level, but it is dotted with hills and low mountain ranges. Towards its edges are areas of grassland. Near the northernmost edge of the forest, on the borders of Guyana and Venezuela, extraordinary rock formations — the *tepuis* — stick up like giant skyscrapers, rising to nearly 9,750 feet high. In the far western Amazon, in Peru and Ecuador, the forest covers the foothills of the Andean mountain range.

Though the rain forest may look the same to us, it contains many different environments. The height of the land, different kinds of soil and rocks, the amount of rainfall, and the flow of rivers have all helped to influence the kinds of plants and animals that make it up. But, by making gardens across Amazonia for thousands of years and planting useful species like Brazil nut trees, Amerindians have also helped to make the forest as varied as it is today.

Amerindians were the first people to live in the rain forest, and it has been used by them for generations, so they have a right to continue to live on these lands. However, the governments of the nine Amazonian countries only officially agree that about 10 percent of the Amerindian lands actually belongs to Amerindians. This is

◀ Although the trees look very similar from the air, the rain forest is varied. Only Amerindians know the names of many of the trees and the habits of the animals there.

certainly true of Brazil, whose borders surround nearly three-quarters of the Amazon forest. Brazil is the only Amazonian country whose government will not give land titles to Amerindians, but other countries question what actually makes up Amerindian land. Many governments have actually encouraged people from other parts of the country to colonize the Amerindian lands. This has happened even where territories have been designated and reserves have been established. A variety of different activities are seriously affecting Amerindian lands today and undermining the culture and life-style of the people.

ROADS

Building roads through the rain forest has had a dramatic effect on countless Amerindian groups. The roads have enabled thousands of people from other regions to move into the forest and settle on Amerindian lands. Colonists burn the forest, frighten the animals away, and bring epidemic diseases like measles, yellow fever, and typhoid.

Roads are often cut straight through Amerindian territories. This happened to the *Waimiri-Atroari* people in Brazil when the road from Manaus to Caracarai was built, reducing their numbers from roughly 3,000 to just 350. When the Trans-Amazonica highway was built across Brazil during the 1970s, it had a similar effect on many Amerindian groups. In the Brazilian state of Rondonia, the paving of the BR364 road is having a devastating effect on 8,000 Amerindians from 40 different groups. Over half a million colonists have flooded in.

▲ Roads cause very serious problems for Amerindians. This new road will allow settlers to invade Amerindian lands in Ecuador.

▲ The destruction of the rain forest to make way for cattle ranching has affected Amerindian groups including the Ashaninka in Peru, the Cuiva in Colombia, the Piaroa in Venezuela, and the Xavante in Brazil.

One of the worst affected peoples is the Nambiquara of the Guapore valley.

RANCHING AND LAND SPECULATION

For the last ten years or so, these have been the chief cause of forest loss. Believing that the forest had no value and the people who lived in it could be pushed aside, governments encouraged wealthy business people and large companies to burn vast areas of forest to show that they now "owned" the land. This land could then be sold for a large profit. Although most of Amazonia is unsuitable for ranching, cattle have been brought in to establish possession of the land and to stop Amerindians from using it.

LOGGING

Much of the valuable tropical timber that we use to furnish our homes is taken from Amerindian lands. Mahogany is being cut illegally from the forest belonging to the Uru Eu Wau Wau people in the Brazilian state of Rondonia. The Chimane in Bolivia have had large portions of their forest destroyed. The Cinta Larga in Brazil have had so much of their forest cut down that they have been forced to accept food from the lumber companies just to stay alive.

AGRICULTURE

In addition to raising cattle, individual colonists and large companies have been encouraged to take over Amerindian lands for small and large

14

scale agriculture. This has caused huge problems for the Amerindian groups affected, and for the poor colonists who have found that they cannot grow the crops they have always grown in the forest soil without the cover of trees. The Matsigenka in Peru have lost large areas to colonists for growing coffee.

DAMS

Plans exist to build a large number of dams across many of the major tributaries of the Amazon River to produce electricity. Several large dams have already been built and 25 others are under construction. Those that are already in place, like Brazil's biggest, the Tucurui, have been a disaster both for the environment and the people living near them. Flooding huge stretches of land has drowned thousands of animals and caused rotting vegetation to give off hydrogen sulfide and methane gas. The lives of Amerindians have been ruined. The Balbina dam north of Manaus submerged a large part of the Waimiri-Atroari's hunting and fishing grounds.

Amerindian Land and the World Economy

The lands of Amerindian communities are fundamental to their way of life. Their identity springs from their relationship with every aspect of those lands and with the plants and animals that they support. They believe that the earth cannot be owned and that people are the guardians of the land they live on.

The governments of the countries in which Amerindians live believe in the principles of private property and selling things that have become commodities like minerals and timber for profit. This is called capitalism. This way of thinking controls the way in which nearly all countries in the world interact. So decisions made by the governments, businesses, and banks of rich nations like the U.S., Britain, and Japan affect how the land in Amazonia will be used.

For example, a rise in the price of oil might make it profitable to start drilling for oil in Waorani territory. A fall in the price of diamonds might postpone a mine in the forests of the Macuxi. This is why it is so difficult for the Amerindians to protect their lands, in spite of the national laws and international agreements that are supposed to keep them safe.

◄ The Itaipu dam on the Parana River. Apart from flooding lands, the lakes created by the dams provide a home for malaria-carrying mosquitoes. The Parakana have suffered badly from malaria, its chills and fever.

OIL

The production of two different kinds of oil is threatening Amerindians, in Ecuador especially. There the activities of several well-known petroleum companies have forced communities of Waorani, Quichua, Cofan, Siona and Secoya to leave their land. Oil companies have caused serious pollution, and their roads have encouraged colonists to enter Amerindian areas.

Meanwhile, enormous plantations of African oil palm have been established on Amerindian lands in Ecuador. This palm tree is grown for the oil its fruits produce, which is now an ingredient of many soaps, shampoos and margarines. Lands belonging to Secoya and Siona groups have been ruined by African oil palm plantations.

MISSIONARIES

Catholic and Protestant missionaries are active across the Amazon. Without being invited, they have settled among hundreds of Amerindian communities. By devaluing their culture and saying that their traditional beliefs are evil, they have persuaded many Amerindians to change their entire way of life. Groups who have suffered very badly from the effects of missionaries include the Panare of Venezuela and the Yuki of Bolivia.

TOURISM

Although tourists may believe that they are helping the people they visit when they go on holiday, they often do more harm than good. Amerindian groups such as Yagua and Witoto communities in Peru have abandoned their traditional way of life in order to dress up and dance for tourists. They say they feel like slaves or animals and dread tourist visits. They have said they do not want to become a sideshow for people from other places.

MILITARY PROJECTS

If the Brazilian government's Calha Norte project

▲ A section of the trans-Amazonian oil pipeline in Ecuador.

goes ahead as planned, the lives of up to 60,000 Amerindians from 83 territories will be changed forever. This major program of military occupation, colonization, and development would cover 14 percent of the Brazilian Amazon, including the border area with Colombia, Venezuela, Guyana, French Guiana, and Suriname. Some of Brazil's largest Amerindian areas, belonging to the Tukano, Yanomami, Macuxi, and Ticuna, might be wrecked by colonists and by other agricultural and industrial development programs.

MINING

Amerindians are suffering greatly because of two different kinds of mining activities: large-scale projects which are part of government development schemes and mining carried out by individuals.

The huge Grande Carajas project in eastern Brazil is concentrated on a vast deposit of iron ore, used to make steel. But it also includes tin, gold, nickel, manganese, and copper mines as well as hydroelectric schemes and agricultural developments. About 13,000 Amerindians, including the Guaja, the Parakana, the Gavioes, and the Xicrin-Kayapo, are affected.

Many other groups have had their lands invaded by individual prospectors, known in Brazil as *garimpeiros*. About 45,000 *garimpeiros* recently invaded the lands of the 9,000 Yanomami in northeastern Brazil. You can find out in detail what effect they have had on pages 18 to 21.

These are the major threats to Amerindian lands today. By trying to protect their lands Amerindians are also trying to safeguard their way of life.

You can find out in detail what effect they have had on pages 18 to 21.

The World Bank

The World Bank and the International Monetary Fund (IMF) have enormous power to affect what happens to Amerindian lands. They lend countries money, often millions of dollars, to pay for huge development projects such as dams. These projects are often destructive, but the banks often ignore the rights and needs of the indigenous people.

▲ This open-pit iron ore mine at Carajas was once covered with tropical rain forest.

The Yanomami

4

▲ A *yano*, the traditional house of the Yanomami.

In Brazil the general laws or principles that the government must follow are set out in the country's constitution. The Brazilian constitution acknowledges the Amerindians' right to their land. However, the government has allowed Amerindian lands to be trespassed on or stolen by other people. The government organization for Amerindians, FUNAI, which has in the past been dominated by the military, has continually put off the demarcation of traditional lands, and refused to punish or remove the people who have invaded them.

Most of the people who have power in Brazil, such as politicians, police and army officers, and ranchers, resent Amerindians and would rather they were not there at all. They think that

> The ban on settlement on Yanomami lands is flouted daily by settlers, backed by the army and mining conglomerates. Already one third of Yanomami territory, rich in gold, diamonds, and bauxite, is subject to applications for prospecting and working rights by companies, including Anglo-American and British Petroleum. (*Independent*, 26 April 1988.)

the Amerindians are inferior and feel that they and others are justified in taking Amerindian land. Despite the constitution, very few people in the Brazilian government have ever been willing to defend Amerindian rights. The case of the Yanomami shows this very well.

The Yanomami's territory straddles the border between Venezuela and Brazil. On the Brazilian side roughly 9,000 Yanomami occupy an area of 23.2 million acres. In 1985 the President of Brazil agreed to recognize this area officially as the "Yanomami Park," and a decree was signed. But nothing was actually done to protect it.

In 1988 the Brazilian government tried to reduce the park's area to about 7.4 million acres, divided into nineteen separate reserves, by issuing another decree. This was against the constitution and its effect was genocidal. It meant that 70 percent of the Yanomami's territory would not be recognized and would be open to invasion. The nineteen reserves would be impossible to protect. The Yanomami and

The *garimpeiros*, working from dawn to dusk, attack the riverbeds and banks with high pressure jets of water. The mud is pumped over a primitive sluice table, which separates the gold from the sludge. The sluice tables recover only two-thirds of the gold, meaning that close to half a billion dollars worth of gold was lost last year.

Evaporated mercury finds its way into the environment. In other regions of Amazonia, it has already entered the food chain.

The *garimpeiros* move slowly upstream until the seam is exhausted. In the process, they silt up and kill the stream. (*Financial Times*, 17 December 1988.)

▼ Amerindian lands are under threat of invasion by colonists such as these building homes in Ecuador.

activists around the world tried hard to get this decision reversed, but, while the government stalled for time, thousands of gold miners flooded on to Yanomami land. Because the miners did not know — and did not care — where recognized Yanomami land was, they went wherever they wanted to.

In October 1989 the federal court ruled that the miners should be made to leave Yanomami land, but no effective action was taken. In January 1990 the federal police were ordered to evict the miners, but the operation was called off after twenty-four hours. One of the main reasons for this was that Romero Juca, the powerful Governor of Roraima (the Brazilian state in which many of the Yanomami live) had encouraged the miners to move on to Yanomami lands in the first place. He had made his dislike of Amerindians well known and wanted the miners — who out-numbered the Yanomami by about five to one — to vote for him in the coming elections.

In 1990 the government actually declared that the miners should be allowed to stay roughly where they were, but work within three mining zones within Yanomami territory. Many miners refused to move. By this time the Yanomami were suffering terribly from the introduced diseases. Their gardens, riverbanks, and many areas of forest had been destroyed. Streams and

---

Romero Juca Filho, the governor of Roraima and an outspoken ally of the miners, has convinced the Ministry of Mines that the prospectors, who produce three tons of gold a month, should stay. Mr. Juca, a presidential nominee and former head of FUNAI, who initiated a policy of selling off timber and natural resources on the Indians' land to pay for their upkeep, has undergone a judicial inquiry into his allegedly corrupt dealings with timber firms.
(*Independent*, 1 August 1989.)

President Collor has finally obeyed the Brazilian court decision and revoked former President Sarney's illegal decrees which divided Yanomami territory into 19 'pockets' and created three illegal mining reserves. But. . . Collor announced he was setting up a group to study Yanomami boundaries. He has given the group six months to do this which is clearly a stalling tactic. (*Survival International Urgent Action Bulletin*, May 1991.)

fish had been polluted with mercury, which is used in the gold mining process. Much of their game had been shot or frightened away. And at least 1,500 of them were dead. All this, because the Brazilian government broke the promises made in its own constitution, which recognizes the Yanomami's rights to their lands.

Davi Yanomami is a famous activist for the rights of his people. He recently sent this message to all people who are concerned about the fate of the rain forests and their people:

The Government treats us like animals, it does not respect us. It takes our lands, on which we have lived for many generations before the arrival of the white man. The invasion of our lands is causing much suffering; our rivers, our forests are disappearing. The Government wants us to abandon our customs and our language and does not want us to own our lands.

I am afraid that our children and grandchildren will suffer even more if we cannot fight to defend and save the life of our people. I am doing all I can to defend my people. Many are dying of the white man's illnesses, against which we have no resistance.

The president promised that he would remove the garimpeiros, but he has done nothing. He does not want to allow our territory to have legal boundaries. Many of our people have been taught to drink cachaca (cane-sugar brandy) which is lethal to them. The prospectors are taking over completely, they are building houses, killing our people and acting as if they owned our land.

We would so much like white people to understand why the preservation of these hills is so important to us. We want white people to help us defend our lands, to work side by side to preserve our way of life.

I, Davi Kopenawa Yanomami, want to help white people learn how to make a better world together with us, for our mutual benefit.

◄ Davi Yanomami has received international recognition for his efforts to protect the forest and its people.

5 Beliefs and Values

Nobody knows exactly how long Amerindians have been living in the forest, but it is certainly thousands of years. An indication of this is the large number of languages that different peoples speak and the great variety of customs they have developed.

Hundreds of different languages are spoken in the Amazon. Some are only known to a handful of people, like the Nahua, who have been reduced to only a few individuals since their first contact with white people in 1984. Some Amerindians speak several languages.

The kind of houses people live in, items that they make and use, and different ways of dressing also express the identity of Amerindian peoples, just as they do for us. The variety and richness of Amazonian cultures demonstrates the very skillful way in which different peoples have

◀ Differences in traditional dress and body decoration show what people in the same group do, and distinguish one group from another.

▲ An entire village uses this Mehinaku house. Other Amerindians live in individual family homes.

adapted to their forest environments. While some, like the Quichua, live in single family houses, others, like the Mehinaku of the Xingu région, build enormous communal houses that are cool and dark inside.

Distinctive face and body decorations also distinguish different peoples and mark the age, sex, and status of individuals, especially on ceremonial occasions. The way in which groups organize themselves — for example, what sort of rules they follow about marriage or resolving quarrels — and the beliefs they hold about plants and animals all vary, too.

SHARED BELIEFS

Most forest peoples see themselves as distinct and separate from their neighbors. But all share important beliefs about themselves and their environment, which unite them and make them unlike Westerners in several ways. The most important idea, central to Amerindian life, is that they share their environment with the animals and plants that make it up. They try hard to conserve it because they depend on it for almost everything and because they believe that it is not theirs to destroy. Underlying this view is the traditional belief that every individual has

Within each Amerindian group or village, people work together as a team. Everyone is free to make suggestions about things that will affect the community. No one is thought to be less important than anyone else. Everyone is involved in producing food, caring for children, and learning songs and stories.

The only person in the community who performs any special activity is the shaman, who links people with the spirit world. Amerindians believe that if people are greedy or show disrespect, this will upset the spirits and make them angry. In retaliation they may make people ill or bring misfortune. The shaman must bring harmony by contacting the spirits and appeasing them.

◄ A Yanomami shaman with a wad of tobacco leaves in his mouth.

a special relationship with the creatures of the forest and rivers during one's lifetime, which forms one's personality and influences the things one does.

To Amerindians, each part of the natural world around them can embody a spirit. Amerindians can communicate with these spirits by dreaming or smoking tobacco or other plant substances. They can find out important information, for example, what has made a person ill or how many animals they can hunt on a particular day. The Amerindians believe that you cannot take something from nature without

making up for it somehow. Overhunting, for example, will anger the spirits who control game animals, because it means that the balance between the numbers of animals and people will be upset. This anger will cause the hunter and his family to be ill.

Most groups believe that some of their ancestors were turned into familiar animals, or rocks, or stars, long ago when the world was very new. The stories and myths about these times remind people that they must respect their environment. The forest is full of spirits that were once people.

MYTHS AND MESSAGES

The Matsigenka live in southeastern Peru. They believe that they were originally made out of pieces of wood. The powerful creator spirit Makineri cut sturdy saplings into lengths and brought them to life by singing and breathing on them. In one of their most important myths, they say that long ago the moon came down from the sky in the form of a handsome man, wearing a yellow feather crown. At that time the Matsigenka had no proper food and ate only mud!

The moon gave a girl cooked manioc tubers, like long potatoes, and other plants, including maize and yams. He married the girl and their four sons became important stars in the heavens, including our own sun. The moon went back to live in the sky, but before he did, he showed the people how to grow the manioc plants he had brought, which he called his daughters, and told the people to care for them well. The Matsigenka believe that the moon watches over all his daughters, and the manioc plants complain to him if people tread on them or do not prepare them in the right way.

All Amerindians believe sharing food with other people is one of the most important things they can do. It would be very bad manners to catch a fish and eat it all yourself, even if your friend had caught one just like it. You would give half of your fish in exchange for half of his or hers.

▲ In many Amerindian myths the moon is an important character.

Amerindians work together in many activities. This wild boar meat will be shared between several families.

Amerindian families share food like this all the time and work together in many activities – the women gathering crops from the forest gardens, cooking, looking after children; the men hunting and fishing, preparing new gardens, building new houses and telling the myths and stories told them by their grandparents. Because Amerindians have always worked together as communities and believe that the forest belongs as much to the animals and birds as it does to them, the idea of owning land by buying it with money is strange to them.

LAND FOR MONEY?

Amerindian views are completely opposite to those of many settlers and business people who have been invading their lands. Business people do not think the forest is alive as Amerindians

do, but value timber rather than growing trees and minerals instead of riverbanks.

Many settlers think that Amerindians are lazy. They do not understand that the Amerindians do not need to work in factories or destroy the forest to live comfortably, and are often jealous of the Amerindians' freedom. Many of the poor settlers themselves have been forced from lands they once worked by powerful people who said they were lazy, too. The powerful people and settlers, invading the forest, mostly feel superior to Amerindians and to nature. Their views oppose those of the Amerindians.

"The forest, the soil and the subsoil are sacred places for our people, but in the mind of investors and developers they are only natural resources." (Ailton Krenak, Amerindian leader.)

The Rubber Tappers

There are about 100,000 rubber tappers working in the Amazon rain forest of Brazil. The families of most of these men and women came to the Amazon region around the turn of the century or during World War II. Encouraged by their bosses to work in lands that already belonged to Amerindian groups, conflict was common. But rubber tappers also suffered dreadful treatment and abuses of human rights. During the 1970s and 1980s many rubber tappers were evicted from the forest as ranching and timber businesses bought and destroyed large areas. Colonists also moved into their regions from other parts of Brazil. Spurred on by the brave efforts of leaders like Chico Mendes, who was assassinated in 1988, the rubber tappers began to resist.

Rubber tappers and Amerindians became aware that they should work together to defend the forest and their way of life. This resulted in the formation of the Forest Peoples' Alliance. The Alliance suggested ways of using the Amazon forest that respect the way of life, culture, and traditions of all forest people.

6 European Contact

History has not been kind to the Amerindians of the rain forest. Ever since Europeans set foot on their lands 500 years ago, the Amerindians have been the victims of greed and misunderstanding. Following the arrival of Columbus in the West Indies in 1492, the whole of South America was divided between Spain and Portugal. This was marked by the signing of the Treaty of Tordesillas in 1494. Europeans had decided that they had the right to rule this great "new" world.

There are no records of how many Amerindians were living in the forest when Europeans first arrived. No one could have imagined the immense size of Amazonia, let alone the numbers of people for whom it was home. Recent research suggests that as many as 15 million people could have been living in Amazonia when the Europeans arrived. Archaeologists have found that settlements of several thousand people each once flourished at the mouth and along the lower reaches of the Amazon River.

The first Europeans known to have descended from the headwaters to the mouth of this vast

▲ The modern airport in Rio de Janeiro. The Portuguese first landed here in 1502.

▲ When Europeans first arrived in South America, the whole rain forest was this unspoiled. Now it is being ruined by ranching, mining, road building, and dams, among other things.

river, led by the Spanish captain Francisco de Orellana in 1542, described very large villages extending all along its banks for hundreds of miles. Inspired by reports of the legendary ruler El Dorado, who was said to coat his body with gold dust every day, Orellana had originally set out in search of gold. Like most of the new arrivals to South America, he was obsessed with dreams of sudden wealth.

Such dreams motivated the Portuguese admiral Cabral, who sighted the Brazilian Coast in 1500. Like Columbus before him, he had left Europe in search of the continent of India, from which he hoped to return laden with valuable spices and silks. Following Cabral's landing, the first sustained contact with forest Amerindians was made by the Portuguese along Brazil's Atlantic Coast. Many people lived in this thickly forested area. The sailors could not believe their eyes.

At this time medieval Portugal was a country of many inequalities. Most of its population were very poor, and diseases were commonplace. The Catholic Church was very powerful and influenced what people did and how they thought about the world. The Portuguese were amazed by what they saw of the Amerindian way of life. One of them recorded in a letter to the King of Portugal:

> "Their bodies are so clean and so plump and so beautiful that they could not be more so."

Another wrote:

> "In every house they all live together in harmony . . . They are so friendly that what belongs to one belongs to all."

They were astonished that the people were so healthy, lived so long, and were not embarrassed without any clothes. The reports that began to reach Europe in the sixteenth century excited the imaginations of those who read them. Laws were made banning the printing and sale of books about South America without a special license. The reports described an alternative to life in Europe which was far more attractive. Fearing a revolution, the rich and powerful wanted to keep this information to themselves.

According to their strong religious beliefs, the Portuguese had discovered a world that was unfinished and that needed to be civilized.

◀ When the Portuguese first arrived in Brazil, they were surprised at how healthy the Amerindians were. One of them wrote, "Their bodies are so clean and. . . beautiful that they could not be more so."

▲ Because Amerindian customs such as face painting were so different from those of the Portuguese, they were believed to be uncivilized.

How the Amazon Got Its Name

Not long after the first Europeans traveled to South America in the sixteenth century, a story arose that a fierce tribe of warrior women lived in the rain forest. They were given the name Amazons, since this was the word the ancient Greeks had used for a legendary nation of female warriors who were said to live in Asia.

When Francisco de Orellana sailed down the Amazon, one of his men claimed that fierce, white-skinned women had attacked them with bows and arrows. It was this and similar stories that led to the river being named the Amazon. No evidence has ever been found that such warrior women really existed and there are certainly no fierce fighting women in the forest today.

Because Amerindians were obviously not Christian, the Portuguese decided that they were more like animals than humans. Amerindians were misunderstood right from the start.

The Portuguese and Spanish had come to conquer South America. Their kings wanted resources to pay for expensive wars and to expand their empires. The first commodity, taken in huge amounts by the Portuguese, was the timber of a rain forest tree that produced a beautiful red dye, then fashionable in Europe. It was known as brazilwood, from the Latin word for red. This name came to be used for the whole country of Brazil.

Any feelings of respect or admiration for the Amerindians soon gave way to aggression and greed. Within fifty years 90 percent of them were dead. European diseases were the main killers: epidemics of flu, measles, dysentery, smallpox, and malaria swept through the forest, wiping out entire peoples. Thousands of

Amerindians were also enslaved and died from cruel treatment.

As the brazil wood forests became exhausted, sugar plantations were set up. Amerindians were forced to work in dreadful conditions. Because so many of them died, slaves were brought from Africa to cut the cane and work the sugar mills. Many of the slaves were bought with tobacco, which became a major export of Brazil.

Amerindians were regarded as nothing better than animals, and so they were constantly hunted down. Those that survived were forced to scatter to remote regions of the forest. Over the next three centuries the French, Dutch, English, and Germans also became involved. Amazonia continued to be raided for all kinds of goods: turtle oil and salted meat; plants for medicines, like curare, ipecac, quinine, sarsaparilla and

◄ This man is carrying a sack on his head. His ancestors were brought to Brazil from Africa about 400 years ago to work as slaves on plantations.

Waorani Amerindians from Ecuador dressed in clothing given to them by missionaries. Apart from losing possession of their land, Amerindians have been threatened in other ways. One of the worst influences on them has been that of the missionaries. In the sixteenth century Jesuit missionaries rounded up thousands of Amerindians in Brazil. They believed they could improve their lives and help protect them from exploitation, but the Jesuits actually exploited the Amerindians. Many Christian missionary sects are still active in the Amazon region today.

copaiba oil; flavorings like cacao and vanilla; and wood like rosewood and mahogany.

Enormous areas of Amerindian land were taken and used for plantations — mostly of sugar, cotton, tobacco, and coffee — and for cattle ranching, logging, and mining. To make matters worse, missionaries flocked to the forests intent on converting Amerindians to Christianity. As well as disrupting whole communities, the diseases they brought killed hundreds of thousands of forest people.

Although slavery was officially abolished in 1888, and the different countries that shared the Amazon became independent of Europe by about this time, conditions for Amerindians did not improve. Many of them tried hard to resist the colonists, but they were always defeated in the end.

Industrial developments and the launch of the inflatable tire in Europe in 1885 had a catastrophic effect. In the western Amazon, the sudden demand for rubber brought about the rubber boom. Thousands of poor people flocked to the forests to collect latex from wild rubber trees. Most of them suffered terribly, but Amerindians generally fared the worst. In the

Putumayo region of Peru and Colombia alone, 40,000 Amerindians were killed between 1886 and 1919.

Though the Brazilian government set up the Indian Protection Agency (SPI) in 1910, with the apparent aim of defending Amerindian lands and way of life, the SPI soon became corrupt. More and more settlers were allowed to flood into the forest in search of minerals, timber, and pastureland, and the SPI sold large areas to speculators who lived in other parts of Brazil or in Europe or America. Well-armed expeditions planned in advance to murder Amerindians in order to steal their lands. In some cases they were left poisoned food and clothes infected with diseases or actually bombed from the air. A few dedicated individuals, like the Brazilian Villas Boas brothers, who set up the Xingu National Park in 1961, tried to intervene. But the government's actions later forced them to give up their work.

In 1968, the SPI was replaced by FUNAI in Brazil. Sadly, although its new President is sympathetic to the Amerindians, FUNAI has mostly been run by the Brazilian military and has not supported Amerindian claims to their land. Instead, like the government agencies of many other Amazonian countries, it has tried to force Amerindians to integrate with white society. This has meant losing their land and their traditions and often their lives. But Amerindians are now demanding the right to choose their own future and control their destiny themselves.

▲　In many Amazonian countries military personnel have had the power to take over Amerindian lands.

Amerindian Response

"Indian wealth lies in customs and communal traditions and land which is sacred. Indian demands should be heard . . . Indians today want political power." (Mario Juruna, Amerindian leader, 1985.)

People who do not live in the rain forest often try to make excuses for what has happened to Amerindians. They say that they needed to be "civilized" and their forest "developed," and because of this their suffering cannot be helped. But this is not how Amerindians see their past or plan their future. They know that everyone on earth has human rights, including being allowed to have their own beliefs and not be oppressed by others. Amerindian groups and individuals have been struggling for five centuries to make their voices heard, but they have recently begun to have much more success. Within the last ten to fifteen years, many Amerindians have begun to organize and stand up for their rights.

The first forest people to form an organization were the Shuar of Ecuador. In 1964 they formed an organization which represented the 20,000 people of all the Shuar communities. In spite of

▲ The men of a Kayapo community meet to discuss their plan for action.

▲ Mario Poyanawa (seated) with his family. Mario is the Union of Indian Nations representative for the Jurua Valley in Brazil.

constant harassment from colonists, they have achieved a great deal: the legal recognition of communal lands, a radio school system that can reach children in very remote regions, and air travel. As Amerindians began to feel less overwhelmed, many indigenous organizations were formed during the 1970s, especially in Peru, where 100,000 forest Amerindians live today. The peoples represented here included the Amuesha, the Ashaninka, the Shipibo and the Aguaruna-Huambisa.

Because so many organizations were formed, the Indian Council of South America (CISA) was created in 1980 in Peru. In 1984 COICA, the Coordinating Body for the Indigenous Peoples' Organizations of the Amazon Basin, was formed. Today, COICA represents the national organizations of five Amazon countries: Peru, Bolivia, Ecuador, Colombia, and Brazil. Each of these countries has set up one national organization to represent some or all of its forest peoples' own, local groups. This means that even a very small community of Amerindians can make its voice heard.

From COICA's office in the Peruvian capital, Lima, the problems and views of Amerindians can be communicated easily to people all around the world. Representatives can travel to national and international meetings to enable Amerindians to be heard and get support. The most important aim of most Amerindians is gaining official recognition of their lands and stopping their lands from being invaded. They know that being in control of their land is the only way to make sure that they can choose their way of life and that their traditions will survive.

They want to represent themselves in any discussions about the future of their forest home. This point is very important. It is the principle of self-determination.

Until very recently, all Amerindians in Brazil were legally considered to be minors. This meant that the government decided they were like children, and they weren't allowed to vote or make decisions for themselves. However, since 1988 they have been regarded as full citizens and the new constitution guarantees them possession of the land they have always lived on. In 1983, Mario Juruna, a Xavante, became the first Amerindian to be elected a member of the Brazilian Congress. He served until 1986. Today, a member of the Terena nation, Jorge Terena, is special advisor on indigenous affairs to the Environment Secretary of Brazil.

Another activist for Amerindian rights who has become well known around the world is from the Krenak people. Ailton Krenak is the National Coordinator of the Brazilian Union of Indian Nations (UNI). He worked with the famous rubber tapper leader Chico Mendes to promote the idea of an alliance between rubber tappers and Amerindians. Today, this alliance — of which Ailton is the president — unites nearly 100,000 rubber tappers and other traditional forest settlers with many of the Amerindians of Brazil. Ailton is now a member of Brazil's new National Council on the Environment, and this means he can vote on environmental issues that concern Brazil.

Amerindians have been active in many different ways, individually and in groups. They have been explaining that their traditional way of life safeguards the Amazon rain forest because it protects the trees. The president of Colombia recently agreed in public that this is so. In October 1989 he announced that 45 million acres of forest (half of the entire Colombian Amazon) had been handed back to the 70,000 Amerindians who live there. Now communities are being helped to set up their own health and education programs. Although the surface of the lands belongs to these Amerindians, the government does not admit that anything beneath it — like minerals and oil — is theirs.

Because so many people all over the world now want to save the Amazon rain forest, Amerindians are trying hard to get a simple message across. This is that much of the forest is rightfully theirs, and if they are allowed to live in it they will make sure it is protected forever.

▲ One of the best-known Amerindian activists, Ailton Krenak, during a visit to Great Britain.

Altamira

In February 1989, the world's attention focused on the small town of Altamira in the Brazilian Amazon. It was there that the Kayapo had called a meeting of Amerindians and the world's press, to protest against plans to build two huge dams near the town. The extracts below tell the story of their struggle:

In 1988 a group of Kayapo Indians launched an extraordinary campaign to halt the construction of the Babaquara and Kararao dams, which threatened their territory at Altamira on the Xingu River. Their leaders visited the headquarters of the World Bank to request the withdrawal of a U.S. $500 million loan. [This led to two Kayapo chiefs, Paiakan and Kube'i, and an American anthropologist, Darrell Posey, being charged with interfering in matters of national security.] They met U.S. senators, toured European capitals, talked to members of parliament, and explained their concerns to environmentalists and human rights groups. Then in February 1989, at the site of the proposed dam, the Indians convened an international meeting. The fate of the Altamira dam had become international news. *(The Gaia Atlas of First Peoples,* 1990*)*

More than 500 Indians arrived at the meeting in close formation, singing war songs. They sat on the floor but frequently rose to their feet for a war dance. The Indians say the dam will drown the rain forest and disrupt their lives.

. . . the Indians accused the planning director of the state electricity authority, Mr. Antonio Nuniz Nobes, of "coming in by stealth" and of "lying." Mr. Nobes, looking scared, explained that the proposed Kararao Dam at Altamira was still in the planning stage and said that environmental studies would be made. (*The Guardian*, February 22, 1989)

The hundreds of Indians [at the meeting] represented all of the 14 Kayapo communities, the six other Indian groups of the Xingu Basin,

▲ Paulinho Paiakan, one of the organizers of the Altamira gathering, outside the British Houses of Parliament.

▲ Amerindians arrive at Altamira to protest about plans to build dams on their lands.

more than 40 other Brazilian Indian nations, and groups from Canada and the United States. Messages of goodwill were sent from, among others, the forest people of Malaysia.

Official government maps had shown six major dams to be built in the Xingu Basin, but by the time the gathering began, discussion had narrowed down to two. These were Kararao, to be built some 79 miles downriver from Altamira, which would flood 297 square miles including portions of the Juruna and the Xicrin-Kayapo Indian areas and even part of the town of Altamira itself and Babaquara, located immediately upriver of Altamira, which would flood an area

of 957 square miles, with portions of the Arara, Asurini, Parakana, Arawete, and Kararao-Kayapo Indian areas. . .

So, what was accomplished [by the meeting]? First (and this does seem final and irreversible), the Federal Court of Appeals has thrown out the charges against Paiakan, Kube'i and Posey, referring to them as "ridiculous." Second — and this could, perhaps, not be final — the government announced it would abandon the Babaquara dam and go ahead only with Monte Belo, [the new name for Kararao].

Soon after the World Bank called off its funding of Amazonian dams. (*Survival International*, 1989)

The Way Forward

Although many problems still exist, the Amerindians are taking the initiative to solve them. Throughout the forest they have been forming organizations to try and ensure that their rights to land and their way of life are recognized and to determine their future for themselves. As part of this process, they have been putting forward important ideas about how the forest can be safeguarded and how some of the damage that has been done both to the forest and to their traditions can be repaired.

A STRATEGY FOR THE FOREST

In Brazil, the Forest Peoples' Alliance has developed a strategy to protect the Amazon rain forest which it would like the government to adopt. The main points are:

• No more rain forest should be destroyed for any reason.

• All big project plans, for example roads, dams, resettlement, mining, exploration and industrial development, should be halted and alternatives found.

• Everything possible must be done to protect the forest that is left and to regenerate or regrow what has been destroyed. The Alliance says that this should be done using the knowledge and expertise of traditional forest dwellers, using Western science and technology as a back-up.

• Forest people should be able to take part in government.

• Ways should be found to help colonists who are already living in the forest to live there without damaging it any more.

The Alliance has suggested ways of making sure that these things can be done. All indigenous

▲ About ten percent of the Amazonian rain forest has already been destroyed, mostly by fires and logging.

areas should be marked out urgently and the lands of rubber tappers and *caboclos* should be recognized. Colonists should be helped to learn from forest peoples how to use the forest and be given collective titles to their land. The government should make sure that no more people need to come to the forest looking for a home. The Forest Peoples' Alliance would also like support to help it coordinate the protection and management of the huge Amazon region of Brazil.

Across Amazonia groups of Amerindians have been setting up and running a variety of projects and programs. The Indian Research Center was set up near Goiania in central Brazil in 1989. It is a base where Amerindian environmental

◀ These Poyanawa and *caboclo* men have been working on the land they share. Cooperation between Amerindians and others would ensure the survival of the rain forest.

knowledge and traditions can be studied and then put into practice in different ways. In 1991 eleven students from the Xavante, Kaingang, Ticuna, Surui, Krenak, Yanomami, Terena and Pankaruru nations attended the center. The students were studying different ways of managing the forest along traditional lines and looking at practical ways of helping their forest to regrow where areas have been cut down by others. They have also been looking at the possibilities for developing products to sell. Activities include making a nursery of forest plants, fish farming, and raising wild animals to release back into the wild. Students have also been studying biology at the University of Goias and law at the new Center For Indigenous Rights in Brasilia.

Pilot projects have been designed among the Xavante and the Surui and others are planned for the Ticuna, Yanomami and Krenak people. The idea is that they will serve as models for

A Declaration of Indigenous Rights

Evaristo Nugkuag is one of the new champions of the Amazon. As the president of COICA, he represents about a million Amerindians and has been active on their behalf in Europe and the USA.

One of COICA's most important tasks has been to try and persuade the United Nations (U.N.) to acknowledge the special rights of forest people in the Amazon. COICA wants the U.N. to proclaim a Declaration of Indigenous Rights. This would provide a moral incentive for governments to acknowledge their right to their traditional lands and to control their future for themselves.

▼   Amerindian leaders speak at a meeting to discuss the threats to their land.

Severia Xavante with dried fruit processed at the Indian Research Center in Brazil.

other communities, showing ways for them to become economically independent while keeping their traditional relationship with their environment.

The work of the Indian Research Center has important implications for the colonists in the forest too. It has already helped one community in the state of Pará to learn how to grow crops on rain forest soil — organically, without chemical fertilizer — and to become self-sufficient. More centers are planned for other parts of Brazil.

The HIFCO Project, near Pucallpa in Peru, is working along similar lines. It is helping families and communities to set up gardens using traditional methods and organizing courses and workshops so that the knowledge of different groups can be exchanged.

Most Amerindians have never had the opportunity to receive medical treatment for the illnesses they cannot cure themselves, or to benefit from any aspect of Western education. In Brazil the Forest Peoples' Alliance has been working to create education programs that are appropriate to Amerindian needs. These aim to strengthen their knowledge and traditions, and explain useful features of Western culture. In

43

Sao Paulo the Embassy of the Forest People has started teaching city children about the rain forest way of life.

Amerindians already know which forest plants will cure them of certain illnesses, but they are now finding ways of integrating certain Western medicines with their traditional practices. The AMETRA project in Peru has been particularly successful and now has government support. Started by a shaman from the Shipibo people, the project, which trains health workers and runs courses and workshops, is combining aspects of Western and traditional health care. The Amerindian groups of the region, including the Ese Eja and Wachipaeri, as well as non-Amerindian communities, can now benefit from an acceptable standard of health care. A women's program has also been started.

Whether raising tapirs or making radio programs, improving their health or selling forest fruits, the Amerindians are reinforcing their self-reliance and cultural identity. One important battle they are still trying to win is to get some of the biggest conservation groups around the world to fully understand their message and to cooperate with them. At the summit meeting held with conservationists in 1990 in Peru, COICA explained their strategy for protecting the Amazon rain forest. In their view the best way of defending the Amazon is to defend the territory of forest people. The environmentalists said they would join forces with Amerindians to protect the forest and signed the Iquitos Declaration which recognizes their land rights and their leading role as guardians of the forest. But many conservation groups still prefer to

▲   The Amuesha from Peru were one of the first Amerindian peoples to form an organization to defend their rights.

make national parks, reserves, and debt-for-nature swaps.

COICA's famous president Evaristo Nugkuag, an Aguaruna said:

> "We simply have to come together to defend the Amazon or we will lose it."

This is the message that unites us all with the Amerindians of the rain forest. As Ailton Krenak has said:

"We have lived in this place for a long time, a very long time, since the time when the world did not yet have this shape. We learned with the ancients that we are a tiny part of this immense universe, fellow travelers with all the animals, the plants, and the waters. We are all a part of the whole. We cannot neglect or destroy our home. And now we want to talk to those who cannot yet manage to see the world in this way, to say to them that together we have to take care of the boat in which we are all sailing."

Glossary

Amerindians   The first people to live in South America, and their descendants.

Caboclo   Descendant of a marriage between an Amerindian and a settler.

Colonist   Someone who moves to an area that appears to be unoccupied to set up a new community.

Corrupt   Dishonest.

Debt-for-nature swaps   Many South American countries owe a lot of money to richer countries and organizations like the World Bank. Some banks will cancel some of the money a country owes them in return for a promise that a particular area, usually of rain forest, will be protected.

Epidemic   A disease that spreads quickly and over a large area.

Exploitation   Getting some benefit from someone or something; taking unfair advantage of other people.

Garimpeiro   An individual miner or prospector.

Genocide   Deliberately killing a whole group of people such as a nation.

Hydroelectricity   Electricity that is made using the power of water. Hydroelectric schemes often involve flooding large areas of land.

Indigenous   Belonging originally or naturally to a particular place.

Integration   Mixing together with other people. For the Amerindians this has usually meant having to give up their beliefs and way of life.

Manioc   A root vegetable that looks like a long potato. It is the main root crop of Amazonian people.

Minor   Someone who is not legally responsible for himself or herself.

Missionary   A member of a religious group who travels to other parts of the world to try and persuade people, who already have their own beliefs, to think as they do.

Multinational   A large company that has factories or offices in more than one country.

Prospectors   People who search for valuable metals in the ground. In the rain forest this often involves mining or destroying riverbanks.

Radio school   A school in which students listen to their teacher on the radio, instead of being in the classroom. This means that children who live a great distance from the teacher can have lessons.

Regenerate   Grow back to the original state.

Reserves   Areas of country set aside for groups or peoples because so much land has been taken over by others. Sometimes, though not always, a reserve is part of the traditional land of the group or people concerned.

Resources   Materials that can be used to make things. These could include wood for building, and gold for making expensive jewelry.

Savanna   Open grassland in the tropics or subtropics with a few trees and bushes growing on it.

Self-determination   Being able to decide how one wants to live one's life.

Titling   If someone has the legal title to a piece of land, it means that it belongs to them and only they can say what is done with it.

Further Reading

Attenborough, D. *Life on Earth*. Little, Brown, 1979
Attenborough, D. *The Living Planet*. Little, Brown, 1984
Gallant, Roy A. *Earth's Vanishing Forests*. Macmillan, 1991
George, Jean Craighead. *One Day in the Tropical Rain Forest*. Crowell, 1990
Landau, Elaine. *Tropical Rain Forests Around the World*. Watts, 1990
Middleton, Nick. *Atlas of Environmental Issues*. Facts on File, 1989
Miller, Christina G. and Berry, Louise A. *Jungle Rescue: Saving the New World Tropical Rain Forests*. Atheneum: Macmillan, 1991
Stone, L. *Rain Forests*. Rourke, 1989

Further Information

Conservation Foundation
1250 24th St., N.W., Suite 500
Washington, D.C. 20037

The Environmental Defense Fund
Dept. P, 257 Park Ave. South
New York, NY 10010

Friends of the Earth
1045 Sansome Street
San Francisco, CA 94111

Friends of the Earth Foundation
530 Seventh Street, S.E.
Washington, D.C. 20003

Greenpeace
1611 Connecticut Avenue, N.W.
Washington, D.C. 20009

Index

*Numbers in **bold** refer to pictures as well as text.*